FREEDOM FLIGHT
The Origins of Mental Power

Lanny Bassham

Olympic Gold Medalist, World Champion and
Founder of Mental Management® Systems.

Mental Management® Systems, L.L.C.
700 Parker Square Suite 140
Flower Mound, Texas 75028
1-800-879-5079
www.mentalmanagement.com

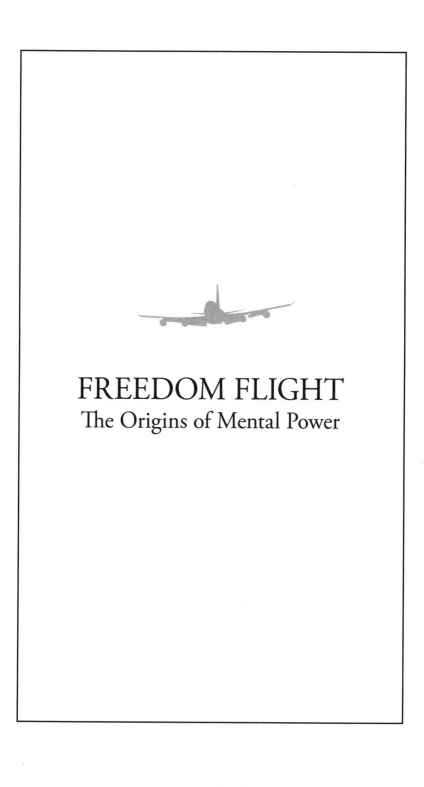

FREEDOM FLIGHT
The Origins of Mental Power

TABLE OF CONTENTS

6 . freedom flight

Acknowledgements

This book is dedicated to the difference makers in our lives, to those who pave the roads so our travel is easier, to those who by their example show us the way, to those who suffer so we do not have to and to those who have given their lives so we might be free. To those who take the time to listen, to advise, to encourage, to console, to empower, to love and to sacrifice so we might find salvation, we give you our thanks.

8 . freedom flight

Foreword

Have you ever experienced a life changing moment; one that stops you dead in your tracks and causes you to reexamine how you have been living your life? This is a story of such a moment. In 1974, I met an incredible person. This is the story of that meeting and of how my life was changed because of it. Because this is one of those "you had to have been there" type of experiences there is no way that I can put you in my shoes so instead I have chosen to relate the experience in a parable. Although the story you are about to read is fiction it is inspired by true events and all of the references to me are true as I remember them. My hope is that you might have a similar reaction to my Jack Sands character as I had to the real events of my life.

10 . freedom flight

The Best Loser in the World

12 . freedom flight

All things considered, it was a good performance for the United States Olympic Shooting Team: a gold medal, a new world record and a silver medal. But I was frustrated; I was the one with the silver.

Now, don't get me wrong. Silver is ten times better than a bronze, and a bronze is ten times better than no medal at all. But in my way of thinking, a silver in the Olympic Games is the very best you can possibly do and still lose.

I had been training for five hours a day, five days a week for fifteen years to prepare for this Olympiad, and now it was over. No one would remember who received the silver that year. Who remembers the silver medalist, the first runner-up to Miss America, and the non-winner of the World Series or the Super Bowl? The only ones who remember are the runners-up, and they can never forget. Left with but two choices, try again or give up, I was determined to continue.

Without the support of the United States Army, I would not have been able to compete in the Olympics. I was completing a three-year assignment at the prestigious United States Army Marksmanship Unit in Fort Benning, Georgia. Commissioned by President Eisenhower to upgrade the marksmanship ability of the Army; the USAMU was world famous as the "Home of Champions". No fewer than five Olympic gold medalists had been developed at this unit, including the winner of my Olympics.

International Rifle Shooting is unique among Olympic sports in that you are trying to make the body stop, instead of making it go. Elite shooters can stop all body movement except the beat of the heart and hold the rifle still enough to hit a ten-ring the size of a teacup at 300 meters. Shooting had been a vital part of my life. I had competed and won on a national level as a junior and collegiate shooter and now my job with the US Army was to win on a global level. Training at the USAMU provided me with the opportunity to become one of the world's elite. The completion of my three year assignment was near. Only one competition remained; the World Military Championships in Cairo, Egypt. Not the Olympics, but important nonetheless. I would be competing against many of the same shooters from the Olympics and there was the special pressure of this perhaps being the last competition of my career. Few shooters are allowed back to the USAMU once they finish their tour. You are expected to serve a variety of assignments as a professional officer in the military and I knew I would never have the luxury of another three-year assignment. Chances were I would never shoot again after this match.

I was thankful for the opportunity that the U.S. Army had provided me, but I was bitter as well. Just when it seemed that I had progressed sufficiently to begin to win for my country the Army was forcing me into retirement without a World or Olympic title. Without a gold medal I felt incomplete. I had not gotten the job done. I felt like the world's best loser.

People would ask me, "Did you compete in the Olympics?"

"Yes, I did."

"How did you do?"

"Silver." I would respond.

"Oh, Who won the Gold?"

I knew I would have to apologize for being second in the world for the next four years and maybe for the rest of my life.

16 . *freedom flight*

The Man

18 . *freedom flight*

The Military World Championships are fired at 300 meters for the rifle event, comprising both slow and rapid fire. Military world titles are awarded in individual events and in team. I had three chances to become military world champion.

I managed to win the trials and secure a trip to the match. The team comprised four shooters and a team captain. It was tradition that we selected the No. 5 shooter in the trials as the team captain, giving us the chance to substitute at the last minute if needed. We were all quite surprised, however, when we were told that this year the team captain had already been selected and we would meet him on the way to Egypt.

If you have ever served in the military, you might relate to the idea that we are often informed as to the logic of certain decisions on a need to know basis. Who was this guy? Why was he going as our captain? What idiot decided to do this to us without consulting the team? One thing I knew for certain, he had better be someone we knew and respected.

Wrong!

On the day of our departure at the airport we were introduced to CDR John Sands USN. I could think of at least four reasons why I didn't like our new team captain. First he was a Navy commander. Navy, can you believe it? I knew only one world-class Navy shooter and it wasn't him. At least he could have been Army or a Marine, but Navy? Second, he didn't know anything about shooting. Where did they get this guy? He was going to be useless, useless, useless! Third, I suspected that he probably heard that we were going to Egypt, had never been there and just wanted a free trip to the pyramids. What were they thinking, and how high up did this guy have connections? But the last straw, the one that really ticked me, was that the team were all sitting together in one section of the aircraft and one of us had to sit with the team captain in another section. Guess who had that honor? Yep, I would be sitting next to him on a 20-hour trip to the other side of the world.

Yuck!

After my request to change seats was rejected, I reluctantly plopped my boiling-with-anger, poor-little-old-me self down in the seat beside The Man.

"Hi, I'm Jack" he said reaching toward me with his outstretched hand. I took it, shook firmly with the confidence that once the introductions were over I could get buried in a book and avoid my seat partner until at least the meal service. Jack was not going to let that happen.

"Well Capt. Bassham, tell me about yourself."

So much for my buried-in-a-book strategy. I launched into what turned out to be a 60-minute autobiography of myself. I told him about my being the worst athlete in school, how I had always loved the Olympics, how I began shooting because it was something that did not require being big, strong or fast. I even told him about my failure at the Olympics, how I had choked under pressure, how scared I was in front of the TV cameras. Adding that I felt I had let my family and country down in Munich, I began to open up to him.

It is amazing! Get people to talk about themselves and you just can't shut them up. I continued pouring out my life story to this guy that I had determined I was not going to like. I told him about my family, about my father who had been a career Army officer and my first shooting coach. I talked about the sacrifices my wife, Helen, had made for my Olympic dream, about not having taken a honeymoon or even a family vacation since we had married. I whined on about how I was not home when our twin sons were born because I was in Europe at a rifle match. He listened without comment as we reached our cruising altitude on the first leg to Cairo.

As this one-sided conversation approached its inevitable end, I suddenly remembered that I was still ticked that this guy was our team captain. He had not said a thing about himself. Well, it was my turn to interview.

"Tell me, sir, how did you get this assignment?"

"I asked for it."

"Really, whom did you ask?"

"The president."

"The president of what?"

"Of the United States of America, of course!"

Talk about high-up connections. I was not certain I believed this.

"You got this assignment by asking the president for it?"

"Yep, I usually get any assignment I want in the military by doing that." OK, now I was certain I didn't believe this.

"Why do you get to do that?" I asked.

"Because he told me to. The president told me that if I ever wanted anything, anything at all, just ask for it.'

"Come again."

"Look, I've never been to Egypt. I wanted to see the pyramids and this seemed like a neat assignment."

Which reminded me, I was upset at his assignment. I could have decked him. It was just as I had thought; a freeloader and at our expense. If you want to go on a vacation, pay for it yourself buddy, I thought.

"Perhaps I should explain," he said.

"Yeah, really, did you finance the president's campaign or something?" I said, forgetting he was my superior officer and how ridiculous a statement I had just made.

"No. Perhaps my pull with the president can best be explained because I spent six years and seven months in a North Vietnamese prison."

In that one sentence Jack Sands indicted, tried and convicted me. I wanted to crawl into a hole and die. No, on second thought, dying was too good for me. Buried alive sounded about right.

"Sir, I apologize. I feel so stupid. No, I am stupid," I said.

"No, you have a right to be upset. I rather enjoyed playing you a bit though. I apologize as well."

Talk about knowing just the right thing to say and at the right time. Now, I felt a bit like someone pardoned of my crime, still guilty but forgiven.

"Is prison something you can talk about?" I asked, remembering that my father could never talk about his

160 days of continuous combat in Italy in WWII.

"I have to talk about it. That's why I was shot down and imprisoned."

"Say again."

"Look, Lanny — can I call you Lanny?" I nodded. "Everything that happens in your life doesn't just happen. There is a plan to it, if you just open you eyes and see it. Do you understand what I am saying?" I nodded the other way this time.

"Let's go back a bit. Seems we have time. This is a long flight. Perhaps there will be time for me to explain about the plan and the bamboo box," he said.

Confused but fascinated, I listened intently.

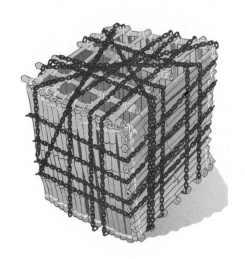

Are You in Prison or Free?

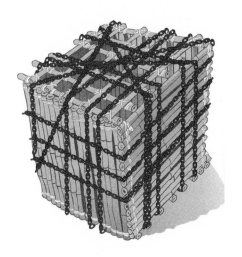

"Are you in prison or free?" He asked.

"Free," I said immediately.

"Are you sure? From listening to you talk, it doesn't sound like freedom. Sounds like you have a pretty strong box around you, keeping you from being free!"

"I'm confused."

"Yeah, you are. So was I until I understood the lessons of the box."

"What's this box you are talking about?"

"Prison, self-imposed prison. OK, let's begin at the beginning. Can I tell you about my capture and imprisonment?"

"Please. Were you in a bamboo box?"

"Yes, for what seemed like a very long time, then later in a cell for a much longer time. This is really not about me, Lanny; it is about you. You don't see that do you?"

"Not yet."

"OK, do you have something to write with and some paper?"

I grabbed my planner and a pen. Feeling I was about to learn something important, I began to take notes.

"Let's talk about the Plan. First, you must continually separate the important from the unimportant in life, thinking about and acting on the important while letting the unimportant go. What happens to you in life is not part of the Plan and is not important. What you do about what happens to you is the Plan. What you think about after something happens to you is the fabric of the Plan. The quality of this fabric shapes the quality and worth of your life, your attitude about yourself and

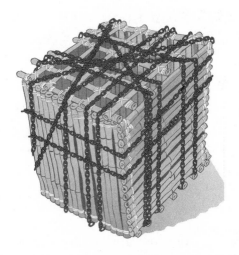

First, one must continually separate the important from the unimportant, thinking about and acting on the important while letting the unimportant go.

your life purpose. I didn't understand this until I lost my freedom in Vietnam. I was in prison for a long time before I was shot down, I just didn't know it. You can live a purposeful life according to a plan or simply be imprisoned by the life your environment gives you. Write this down." Jack said.

Taking my pen I began to record the three principles he had just given me:

> *First, one must continually separate the important from the unimportant, thinking about and acting on the important while letting the unimportant go.*

Everything seemed important to me. I wondered how you knew what is important and what isn't. One thing was for certain: I could not recall ever having tried to separate the important from the unimportant. Also, my thoughts were mostly influenced by my environment. I thought about what my surroundings presented to me — good or bad, positive or negative, important or unimportant. I made no effort to focus only on what was important or to let go of the unimportant. I would just take things in the order life presented them to me and try to deal with them without setting up any kind of priority to them.

> *It is unimportant what happens to you in life. What is important is what you do about what happens to you.*

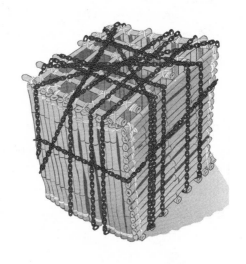

It is unimportant what happens to you in life. What is important is what you do about what happens to you.

Thinking that it was up to me to *make things happen* in my life, I was always worried about everything that happened or didn't happen to me. I constantly compared expected results with actual ones. I measured my worth as a person by what did or did not happen. If I made an "A", I was a superior person. A "C" meant I was average. Jack was saying that not only was I not in control of what happened in my life, but also what happened or did not happen was not important at all.

You can live a purposeful life according to a plan, or simply be imprisoned by the life your environment gives you.

Life has a purpose? Am I supposed to be something or do something? I always thought I was just supposed to pass the class, do my job, keep my nose clean, pay my taxes and die.

As Jack talked, I thought I was beginning to understand what was being said, but I just wasn't sure.

"Lanny, you never really appreciate something until you lose it. I lost the control of my life when my A-6 Intruder was hit by a surface-to-air missile over North Vietnam. I was assigned to Attack Squadron 65 aboard the USS CONSTELLATION. On August 27, 1966, my Bombardier/Navigator, LTJG George Cox and I were on a strike/bombing run when the SAM hit us. Flying at about 3500 feet, the aircraft immediately inverted. The stick was frozen and we were bouncing wildly. Later I learned that our right wing had been blown off. Instinc-

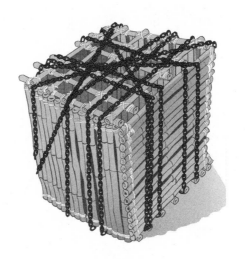

tively, George and I ejected the aircraft."

"The earth hit me HARD. Feeling dazed, I extracted myself from my gear and made my way to a small knoll. I had suffered a compression fracture in my back. Several vertebrae had been pushed together. I saw about 100 people running toward me. When I realized that I was going to be a prisoner, I sat down and pulled out a cigar. Just as I was about to light it, a hand came from behind my head and yanked it from me. My freedom to do what I wanted was over, at least for the next six plus years."

"As the most aggressive of the multitude advanced toward me they could see I posed little threat to them. I was unarmed with an injured back and surrounded. Raising my arms should have signaled submission. I suppose in this village it stands for let the beatings begin. In my final attempt at finding any kind of humor in the situation, I calmly extracted another cigar from my jacket. Unconsciousness followed."

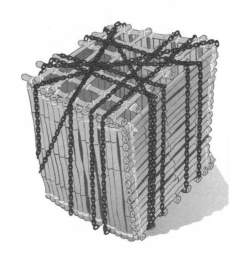

34 . *freedom flight*

The Bamboo Box

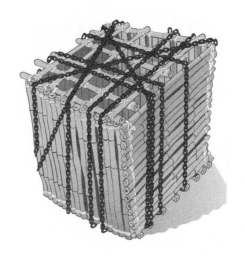

36 . *freedom flight*

"The next thing I remember was intense pain. My elbows were tied behind my back, pulling a shoulder out of socket. My knees were in my chest. I was imprisoned within a 4-foot square bamboo cage, secured by metal chain. Two long poles ran under its top. Later I would learn that these provided my captors with a convenient method of moving me around. I'd seen animals in cages like these in movies but never a man. Why put me in a cage? It didn't make sense because I couldn't move. The compression fracture on my spine would paralyze me from the waist down for a week."

"Turning my head to look around, I felt stubble of beard growth. I'd been out for several days. What do you do with a prisoner that can't walk and vehicles are unavailable? You cage or carry him. It seemed no one wanted to carry me."

"The unconsciousness was a blessing in those first few days. It remitted the intense pain of the ropes. Both of my shoulders were out of their sockets now and if I didn't get some water soon, the cage would become a coffin. Terror hit me as I realized I was completely alone. No one was going to help me and I couldn't help himself. For the first time in my life, I felt really alone", Jack said. "For some unknown reason, my captors had abandoned me. Were they coming back? Or did they intend for me to just die in the cage?"

"Have you ever been lost, Lanny? Really lost and alone?" He asked.

"No!" I said. "Not like that. Not anything like

that."

How could I relate to what he was describing? I'd never been in combat, shot down or captured. Of the graduating seniors in my university ROTC class, four would die in Vietnam. I would never be called to go. Not only had I never been in war, I'd never even been in danger. I couldn't help comparing his life to mine as he continued.

"My primary concern was water. Dehydration had set in. My arms were dysfunctional and the cage was barely large enough to allow me to turnover on my back. What could I do? Without water soon, I would surely perish. What were my options? Calling out was futile. No one could hear me. I was clearly out of options. Nothing to do now but die!"

"When you're near death, no matter how connected you have been to God in the past, your perspective on the eternal changes. We can conveniently avoid talking about the after-life or whatever that means, when we're healthy, safe and occupied with what I call the immediate, unimportant things of life, like hobbies, traffic or TV. When facing death head-on, you're forced to examine your beliefs. Is there a God? What is going to happen to me after I die? If there is no God, I won't care. If He does exist, I'd better care!"

"Do you believe in God, Lanny?" He asked.

"Yes, I am a Christian." I said.

Jack continued, "My mother and father raised me to believe in God, Christ, the Bible, heaven and hell, church on Sundays, Bible school, prayer before meals, the whole enchilada. I believed in God. I just never really needed Him. Not until the box."

"For the first time in my life I had to decide what I believed. Chances were that in a few hours I would meet death. I made a decision. God existed and I needed Him. I prayed for God to hear me. Remembering a passage of scripture, I repeated the words of Jesus on the cross: 'Into your hands I commit my spirit.' Then I relaxed. Peace flowed over me. I was prepared to die."

"At that very moment, it began to rain. The cage was under a tree. The leaves caught the rain, collecting and channeling it, until it ran off the lowest limb of the tree above me and into my parched lips."

"I needed God and he heard my prayer and met my need," Jack said. "Now you can believe what you wish about this. Could have been a coincidence. It rains in Vietnam. Think what you want, but I took it as a clear sign that God wanted me to live for some reason. If not, why not just kill me in the plane crash. No, I was going to survive and I was not alone. I would never be alone again, ever! Temporarily refreshed from the rain, I slept."

"So you feel the box brought you closer to God?" I asked.

"No," Jack said, "God used the box to allow me to find Him."

"Adversity is an effective teacher. Tragedy, like natural disaster with loss of life or war or disease works to cause us to separate what's important from what's not. When we are safe, comfortable and secure, sometimes

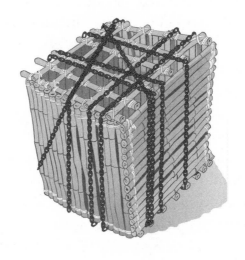

Living without principles is like treading water.
You work hard but never go anywhere.

we start thinking that we are in control of events. We can lose perspective. Then God gets your attention. You must continually separate the important from the unimportant."

"How do you know what is important and what is not?" I asked.

"You'll know when you take your focus off of you. You can't see what's ahead if you're looking at your own feet." He replied.

"Most of our lives we are me centered. This is normal for a child. A child cannot take care of himself. Of all of God's creatures, the human infant is perhaps the most helpless. But as we mature, we must look beyond ourselves. People are important, very important. Relationships are important. You miss that which is taken away. I'd lost all of my relationships except the spiritual. Prison has a way of clarifying thought. The absence of environmental distractions helps to focus the mind on the important things. The principles of survival are very similar to the principles of success. Living without principles is like treading water. You work hard but never go anywhere."

"I began to solidify principles that I would live by." Jack said. "Do you have that pen ready?" He asked.

"Sure!" I prepared to write again.

Everything we experience in life acts as preparation for the future.

"There must have been a reason I survived," Jack said.

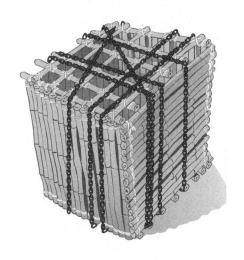

Everything we experience in life acts as
preparation for the future.

"I was being taught something, prepared for something."
Then Jack paused and looking at me he said. "I was preparing to talk to you."

"To me?"

"Certainly, your attitude toward me radically changed when you found out I'd been a POW. My imprisonment has given me a certain power with people. This power is a responsibility I do not take lightly. So, in a way, I survived so I could talk to you today. You're an Olympic Silver Medalist. You must have a certain power over people when they find out about that achievement."

"Actually, I think the gold medalists have all of that kind of power." I said.

"What would you do with the power if you had it?"

"Huh?"

"What if you were Olympic gold medalist? How would you use the power of the position?"

"I ... well!"

"I take it if you haven't given that much thought."

"No. I've been so concerned with the struggle to win the medal I haven't given much thought to being a gold medalist."

Next, Jack gave me a powerful principle.

> *To he who has been given much shall much be required.*

"Everything we do affects someone. The greater your achievement becomes, the greater the possibility of influencing others. That's a responsibility you'd better ac-

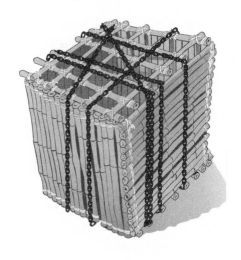

*To he who has been given much shall much
be required.*

knowledge." He continued.

"Alone in the bamboo box I had no influence over anyone. Today, because of my experience, I have influence. It is the kind that cannot be purchased with money. I have something many people desire but I have not met anyone that would choose my way of obtaining it. It is very much like the old saying, everyone wants to go to heaven but no one wants to die! In some very real ways I have been reborn. I am not the same person that was shot down that day. The experience has liberated me. Today I'm free but with far more responsibility than before."

"Are you saying that you are thankful about being in the box?"

"I'd say blessed is more the point. Without that experience, I am quite certain I would still be in prison. The box is not what it appears. Do you follow?"

"You've lost me!"

"OK, I'll illustrate. Draw a box."

I drew four lines in the shape of a box on my pad.

"Now, how many sides does a box have?"

"Four." I said.

Jack pointed to my drawing and said. "When I look at your drawing, I see a square, not a box. Now, draw a box."

This time I drew a 3-D version of my box. It looked a lot like a die with no dots on it. Anticipating a question, I blurted out, "OK, a box has 6 sides."

"Much better, but a real box would have 12 sides: top, bottom, left, right, front and back for the inside and the

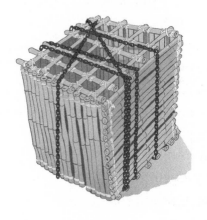

*Your environment is not reality. Your
perception of your environment is reality.*

same for the outside. Is my answer more complete?"

"I would say so, but I really didn't think of it that way."

"That's the point." Jack said. "The way you see things makes all the difference in the world. If you were imprisoned in a box, you would understand the importance of inside and outside. Here is the message:"

Your environment is not reality. Your perception of your environment is reality.

"Some of the most important and wonderful things that happen to us in life seem at the time to be disaster. Saying that prison was a blessing seems strange and must be explained. You see Lanny, the box experience provided the time and solitude to address critical issues about my life. Prior to imprisonment, I never took the time to reflect on anything but what my environment presented to me. If my environment was good, I was happy. If not, then like a weed in the wind, I went along. When hungry, I ate. When sleepy, I found a warm comfortable bed. When lonely, I just called a friend. Everything was provided. I lacked nothing, so nothing seemed really important."

"It's like not really appreciating something until you lose it?" I said.

"Almost! Maybe a clearer way of saying it is that you do not appreciate a thing until you take the time to see it for what it really is. Your environment can mislead you, distracting you away from seeing what is actually happening. We tend to rush through life. Days go by in a blur. We take no time for seeing beyond the surface. We don't really listen to people or appreciate them. At first glance, the box looks like a cell or perhaps a coffin. I would come to know that it would be much more than that. Your environment is what you make it."

"That's why I only saw four sides to my box. I really didn't take the time to look carefully at what you were asking. I just drew the first image that popped into my head," I said.

"Exactly. You chose the answer that required the least amount of time and effort to respond. That is the same way I would have responded prior to the box experience. People pass up opportunity every day because they do not take the time to really see instead of just look. First impressions are rarely accurate as evaluations. I was fortunate. I was forced to stop and take a look at my life. I was given plenty of time alone to evaluate just who I was and why I acted as I did. Most people never take the time to do that. Have you ever thought about why you are living?" Jack asked me.

"No" My voice was barely audible. Everything in my life seemed to be a rush to get somewhere, to finish something or acquire something, never stopping, never evaluating and never taking time to look at why I lived. Rush, rush, rush.

"I still remember vividly the first few days in the box. A man can exist for many days without food if he has water. The rain sustained me and also loosened my ropes so that I was able to free myself of their confinement after a painful struggle. Still barely able to move more than a few inches at a time without agony, I surveyed my situation. There was no hope of escaping the box. Four inch bamboo lashed with chain seemed impenetrable to someone in my condition."

"Early one morning I was jarred awake by someone hitting my cage. My captors had returned. Five VC, who seemed disappointed that I had survived, surrounded me. They seemed more than a little surprised that I was out of my bindings. At first, they tried to remove the metal chains surrounding the box but apparently they did not have the key to the locks. Frustrated, they soon ignored me."

"During the next few days I was fed small amounts of rice and fish and some water to drink. It seemed that they wanted me to live and were confident that I couldn't escape. Then they departed and I was again alone with no food or water."

At that point in Jack's story, the flight attendant came by to ask if we wanted something to drink and to take our food order — chicken or fish. For a moment I felt guilty again. Jack's story was haunting me. I had never known hunger.

"How did you survive without food?" I asked.

"Actually, the survival of the body was not nearly as important as the survival of the mind. Food was not important. My attitude about food was important. If you think about eating and how much you need food, you get really hungry. I could not afford to think about eating, as I had nothing to eat. I determined that I was go-

*Focus only on the solution to the problem
and not on the problem itself.*

ing to be sustained. I did not have to worry about that. That job I turned over to God. My greatest concern was keeping my mind off of the desire to eat and the feelings of fear and despair the environment was creating."

"It is truly amazing! You have to think about being afraid to have fear. You have to consciously think about despair to be desperate. The mind can only think of one thing at a time. If you control that one thing, you control your environment. Your environment cannot control you. When your environment is good, you can afford to relax and enjoy it. But, if it is not good it takes effort to control the picture. What you see determines how you feel about your situation. I learned to control my thoughts one picture at a time. That's when I learned a vital principle of success and survival."

Focus only on the solution to the problem and not on the problem itself.

"Life is full of problems, obstacles, potholes and wrong turns. If we focus on theses things we cannot be seeing the solutions that are always there. Remember, if you take your mind off of the problem you are free to find a way to solve it. So, I chose to think about the solution to my problem. Do you know what that solution was Lanny?"

"I don't think I do." I said.

"I learned that no matter how bad my environment seemed, I could control my attitude about it by controlling my thought picture. My problems were many but my conscious mind could only think about one thing at a time and I could control that one thought. You see, as long as I controlled the next thing that I thought about my environment did not matter. Do you see that?"

"I'm beginning to see, but how did that solve your problem?"

"It didn't solve the problem of being imprisoned in the box, being hungry or being alone. The only solution to my problem was time. You see, sooner or later, the VC had to come back and feed me. Every time they showed up they would move me a little closer to a roadway and at some point I figured that they would get a truck up there and haul me off to prison. I hoped, at that time, I would get better treatment and at least find some companionship. All of these were out of my control. The solution was simple. Control my attitude until the situation improved; just pass the time away. My plan was to replace worrying about my situation with thinking about things that brought me joy."

"What did you think about?"

"Golf."

"What?" I asked.

"Most of the time I thought about golf. Oh, I thought about my family a lot, but that sometimes made me miss them too much but golf did the trick. I love playing golf. I was a pretty good golfer. I had a 10 handicap and had been playing as much as I could ever since high school. My game had a fault though. I was not good at putting the ball. All of the other parts of my game were solid. I just three-putted way too many greens to par a course."

"I vividly imagined hitting thousands of perfect shots off the tee, straight down the fairway. Then I would work on my approach shots. Finally, I would make putts that the pros could only dream about. I played countless hours of golf in that box. I especially worked on my putting game. I kept telling myself that I was getting better and better. I made thousands of perfect putts. At times, I actually found myself enjoying the experience. It took my mind off of my situation and on to something that I really enjoyed doing. The best times were at night when in total darkness I could really feel the club in my hand. I became a much better golfer because of the box."

"Do you mean that by just thinking about doing something that you can improve your ability to do it? That sounds weird to me." I said.

"Do you know what a preset is?" Jack asked.

"You mean like the presets on the radio in a car? You set them to find a certain station when you hit them?"

"Exactly! Well, there are presets in your mind as well. Habits and attitudes that make you act like you. You have an opinion about what you can and cannot do. Here is an example. Finish this sentence. Never talk to _____."

"Strangers." I said quickly.

"Right! That's a preset. You learned that from someone in your family, probably Mom and Dad, and so it is like you to believe it."

However, Jack said, this preset is flawed. If you never talked to a stranger, how would you make friends? Much of what we believe to be true about us is incorrect. Some

54 . *freedom flight*

people think that they cannot do things well, when in fact they find out later in life that they can excel at the task with training and time.

"I had a preset about my putting game," he continued. "By imprinting perfect putts thousands of times in the box, I changed the preset. My attitude changed from 'I have trouble on the green' to 'I putt like a pro.' You see, the mind cannot tell the difference between what you vividly imagine and what you actually do."

"You do not have to be in a bamboo box to change your attitude but you do have to decide that you want and need to change before change can happen. I was in the box long enough for me to reevaluate much more than my golf game. I took a good look at who I was and how I acted and I did not always like what I saw. I had been in prison long before the box and I was beginning to see a way to free my mind from captivity."

"Finally, just as I had thought, one day I was loaded on a truck and hauled off to the Hanoi Hilton. I would spend six years there. There would be countless more hours of golf and reevaluation. I would be inspired and taught by my mates in prison until we were released and headed for home."

"That must have been something!" I remarked.

56 . *freedom flight*

Homecoming

What he remembered most, Jack told me, was the flight out of Viet Nam. A crew member asked him what he had missed most about freedom. They all wanted to be reunited with their families, of course, and to see the USA and how it had changed while they were gone. Then they began to laugh and talk about less meaningful, but still important, things that they wanted to do.

"Like what?" I asked.

"I remember saying that the first thing I'm going to eat is ice cream." Jack said. "I had not eaten ice cream in over six years. The first thing I wanted to buy was a watch. I wanted one with a heavy back so I could have it engraved with the words 'Freedom Flight' and the date we flew out of Viet Nam. But more than anything else I had a terrible urge to play golf. I declared that nothing would keep me from hitting a golf ball on the first course I would see in the USA."

"When we landed in Hawaii to refuel the aircraft we were surprised with a special gift from the crew," Jack added. "That was the first time I had tried to eat ice cream through a flood of tears."

"Our next stop was the USA mainland and a naval base there. When we landed we were met by ambulances to take us to the hospital for tests and observation. I'm certain we looked a sight. Most of us weighed half of our flight weight. When my ambulance arrived I jumped into the front seat with the driver. It was a bit chilly so he offered me his jacket as we made our way to the hospital."

"Then an incredible thing happened. I looked to my

right and I saw a golf course. I told the driver to pull over. I couldn't believe it but he did just that. I jumped out of the ambulance and went into the club house of the course."

"I want to play golf." Jack demanded to the manager. "I can still remember him looking at me in disbelief. I was standing before him in skin and bone, in a jacket that was at least three sizes too big for me and I'm certain he thought I was deranged or homeless or both."

"Are you a member of this club?" He asked.

"Not yet!" Jack said.

"Well, you have to be a member or play with a member here, Sir."

"Are there any members here?" Jack enquired.

"In the bar."

Jack walked into the bar, picked up a fork and a glass tumbler and banged the fork against it to get the attention of four men at a table.

"I'm Lt. Commander Jack Sands, U.S. Navy. I've just spent six years in a North Viet Nam prison camp and this is my first day home. I want to play golf. Would any of you be willing to help me?"

"What do you think happened? These guys were all retired Navy. With tears in their eyes they jumped up and literally carried me to the pro shop. Within minutes I had been outfitted with the finest golf attire known to man and with new bag and clubs in hand we were off to the golf course to play."

"Wow!" I said as Jack's eyes widened and he became excited in the telling of the game.

"On that day, in a severely weakened condition and in new shoes and with clubs out of the box I shot par golf on that first hole. It was truly amazing. My drives were straight down the fairway, just like I had imagined. My approach shots were controlled and online. And my putting, oh my putts were straight and true. My teammates were astonished but somehow I knew it would be like this. I had seen it thousands of times in my mind. It could be no other way. It was just like me to do it. They asked me 'Jack, how could you do that?' I answered, 'It's easy. You see, it's been a long time since I've missed a putt!'"

Jack Sands had come home. I could not hold back the tears as Jack continued with his story.

"A few days later one of the men that I had played golf with picked me up at the hospital. He had remembered that I had wanted to purchase a watch and he said he would take me to do that. I had a few dollars saved as we had received a partial payment of our pay in the hospital but I was cautious not to spend too much because I was going home to my family in just a few days. He said not to worry, as he knew just the place for a good watch. We drove up to a very large jewelry store but I noticed that the sign on the door said closed. This seemed odd to me. It was in the afternoon and in the middle of the week so I asked him about the closed sign. 'Don't worry about it,' he said. 'I own this place.'"

"It seemed like a hundred people were inside. The men I'd played golf with and their families, much of the staff of our wing at the hospital and many servicemen and women that I did not know were there. A big sign hung from the ceiling at the back of the shop that said WELCOME HOME JACK. After the bursting applause the people parted forming a pathway to a group of special people. They had flown in my wife and children for this special reunion. What an amazing group of men and women!"

After the party was well under way, Jack remembered, he was presented with a large green box. When he opened it he saw a solid gold Rolex President wristwatch that had been engraved *Freedom Flight* and the date of his departure from Viet Nam.

"'Now don't worry about any kind of a bill for this watch,' my friend said. 'We took up a collection from some of our Navy buddies. No one was allowed to donate more than $50. We collected so much money we not only were able to cover the watch but we had enough to fly in your family and throw this party.'"

Then Jack took the watch from his wrist and turned it over. I read the inscription and trembled.

Jack's story was incredible. Here was a man who could have been bitter about having six years of his life taken from him, but instead he was finding the positives in the experience. His attitude about his tragic captivity had empowered him in incredible ways.

I sat in total awe of this man. By comparison my challenges were trivial and I'd spent much of my time in recent months feeling sorry for myself. I felt embarrassed, but in a strange way enlightened, because of Jack's story. He had taken away all of my excuses, my self-doubt and my poor-little-me self-talk. At that moment, more than anything else in the world, I wanted the control that Jack Sands possessed over his attitude. I wondered if he could help me to redirect my life.

"Sir, I could really use some advice. I want to be able to use some of the principles you have talked about in my life. Do you think you could help me to do that?" I asked.

"You still don't get it do you? Remember I told you that things don't just happen. You and I are supposed to be at this place and at this time in history so that we can have this conversation. Don't you understand? That's why I survived. I needed to experience a change in me so that I could help you. This has always been about you, not about me. I was shot down in Viet Nam and put in prison then found my freedom for a reason. I know what I'm supposed to do with my life. I'm supposed to help people like you. Do you know what you are supposed to do with your life? Until you do, you are still in prison. The first thing you have to do is to break out of your box. Are you ready to do that?"

"Yes, I am!" I replied. "But, how do I find out what I'm supposed to do with my life?

"The first place to start is to find your passion. What are you passionate about? What are you happy doing?"

"All I've ever really been interested in is competing in rifle shooting and I've just been told that the opportunity will be denied me after this competition. Shooting is one of the most expensive events to train for in the Olympics. I've been successful because I've been assigned to the marksmanship unit and I've been able to train. I don't see how I can do it on my income alone and I don't have the time to train if I am working a normal military job."

"The first problem you have Lanny, is that you are focusing on the problem, not on the solution. You do not have to accept as your fate that what people tell you is always going to happen. My captors told me a thousand times I would never leave Viet Nam and here I am. Those Army assignment officers just might be wrong about you and your chances of getting back to the marksmanship unit. Has anyone ever been reassigned there after having been told that they would never be able to return?"

"As a matter of fact, one of our best shooters was able to return, but it was a unique situation and his chances were slim." I said.

"I can't believe what I'm hearing from an Olympic silver medalist," Jack said. "Tell me about the chances of anyone winning a gold medal in the Olympics. How slim are they? Look, if you are supposed to win an Olympic gold medal, if it is meant to happen, a door will open. Lanny, the world is full of open doors. You will not continue to think about your Gold Medal if there is no possible way for you to achieve it. The more you think about accomplishing a goal the more likely you will see a way to accomplish it. Just because you cannot see the door now doesn't mean that given time you will not find it. Sometimes waiting it out is the answer. Believe me. I know about just waiting for the door to open."

Was my life purpose to compete, or was the process of

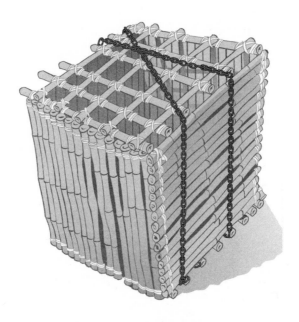

Focus only on the solution to the problem and not on the problem itself. Thinking about problems enhances the tension and leads to a depressed attitude. Solutions empower our thinking and energize us.

competing just preparation for my life purpose? I wasn't sure. What I did know was that the first thing I thought about when I got up and the last thing I thought about before I slept was winning the gold. The medal seemed to call to me. Jack said that I wouldn't think about my goal if a way to achieve it would not appear. Perhaps I could get back to the unit, if not for a full tour, then maybe for enough time before the Olympics to make the team and prepare for the games. I felt like I had a chance, however slim, to reach my dream.

For the first time in my life I began to imagine what I would do if I had an Olympic gold medal. I've always enjoyed teaching, and I thought that I might make a good teacher or a coach. Perhaps I could open an international shooting school and coach future Olympic gold medalists. I wondered if I could take the principles that Jack had given me and use them not only to win my medal, but also to help others. My life purpose was beginning to take shape. The walls of my box were coming down.

"I want to win a gold medal so I can open an international shooting school and train Olympians," I blurted out.

"Welcome to the freedom of living with a purpose," Jack said. "Now, you need to understand that every purposeful life has a plan to it. Once the goals in your life are in sync with that plan good things will begin to happen to you."

"How do I know what the plan is?"

"Your job is not to try too hard to develop the plan of your life purpose. Your job is not to get in the way of

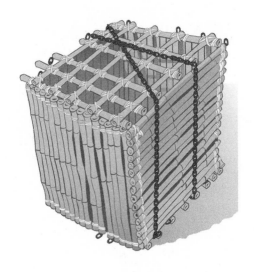

Every purposeful life has a plan to it. Once the goals in your life are in sync with that plan good things will begin to happen to you.

it."

"You're losing me again," I said.

"OK, there is a difference between your life purpose and the goals you set for your life. The level of accomplishment in your life, how much money you earn and how well you can shoot in a competition can be enhanced by setting goals and written plans are valuable in these situations. The plan of your life purpose is not so much what YOU create but more to the point what has been created for you. A life purpose is why we live not how we live. If we are put here by God or we have karma or maybe it is just fate, doesn't it stand to reason that as long as the plan exists we don't have to worry about all of the details. For example, I believe the plan was that I was captured, put in prison and survived so that I might have a special insight into how to help people like you. I had nothing to do with my being shot down, with who found me or how I was imprisoned. I had no control over the fact that I was eventually released. How could I plan any of that myself in advance? This is how most of life purpose plans works out. It rarely happens that things work out exactly how you PLAN them. People who spend too much time attempting to design all aspects of their life end up trying to play God and that just doesn't work, does it?"

"I agree with that," I said.

"There is a plan to the drama of life but we are not the writers of the drama we are merely the actors. Our job is simply to act well and the play will be a success. Do you see that?" Jack said.

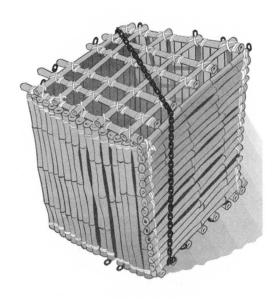

We will not continue to think about a goal if there are not open doors waiting for us to go through that make the goal attainable.

"OK, I think I do. My job is not to try to direct events as much as it is to manage my own participation in the events. Is that right?"

"Right! Your job is to connect with the plan based on what happens to you in life. For example, when I needed water in the box somehow I received it. That let me know that survival was part of the plan. What happens in life will let you in on the details of the plan if you are paying attention. Here is another example. The best medal you could have taken in the Olympics was the silver."

"Why?" I asked.

"You told me that you had a mental failure and shot a score well below your potential. Are you more motivated now to discover the secrets of controlling the mind under pressure because of your inability to win the gold?"

"Of course, if I'd won the gold I probably would have thought I knew everything I needed to know. And, if I'd taken the bronze I don't think I would have been as hungry to learn more about the mental game. I see what you are saying. The silver has made me hungry to learn more. Actually, I know now that it wasn't my time to win. The gold medal was planned for my teammate, not for me. The gold medal was part of his life purpose. Is that right?"

"Yes, but Lanny, you received much more than accomplishing a goal in your taking of the silver medal."

"What do you mean?"

"Attainment is the greatest measure of success, not just accomplishment."

"What is the difference?" I asked.

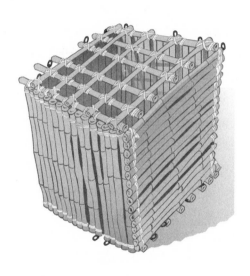

Attainment is the total of your becoming and your accomplishing. The world tends to only measure your accomplishment.

"Accomplishment is how we measure the external. It is easy to measure. It is Gold, Silver or Bronze. It is A, B, C, D or F. It is how much money we are paid or how much our home or car costs. But there is another measurement that is critical to success. It is called becoming. Becoming is how we measure the internal. It is very difficult to measure. Who we become in the competition of life is another measure of success. It's the measure of your knowledge, your character and your growth as a person."

"Attainment is the total of your becoming and your accomplishing. The world tends to only measure your accomplishment. That's why you took it as a failure when you won the silver instead of the gold. Do not forget to credit your becoming when striving for your goals and following your life plan. Sometimes, when looking for one thing we do not find it, we find something better. Your goal was to take the gold, I'm sure, but your life plan was followed more closely by your taking the silver instead. Do you see that?"

"Yes, I see now that I was not mentally prepared to win the Olympics and that's why I had the mental meltdown. I've never wanted something so bad in my life. I had worked really hard for over 15 years for that medal," I said.

"Have you ever thought that maybe you were trying too hard?"

"Hey! The harder you work the luckier you get!"

"I am not disagreeing that hard work is essential for success in any worthwhile goal. I am suggesting that

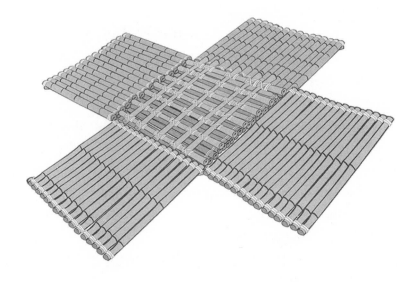

Everything that happens to you, seemingly good or bad, happens for a reason. The reason always has a beneficial component to it if we stop to see it. God endows us with weapons to fight through adversity.

you might have over-tried in the Olympic performance and that might have kept you from winning. What do you think?"

"What is the difference between working hard and trying hard?" I asked Jack.

"Everything we do in life requires a certain amount of mental effort to do it well. When we give a task one percent too much or too little effort our performance drops. There is a time to try hard. It is in preparation, but in execution you must only try hard enough."

Jack was making sense. I needed to find the answers in how to control my mind under pressure. Shooting at elite levels is 90 percent mental but I spent 99 percent of my time and energy on the technical issues. If I knew as much about the mental game as I did about technique I could dominate my sport. I was beginning to see how my life plan could direct my goals. What happens to me is not my concern but what I do about what happens is my concern. I must pay attention to the message that is being sent to me about my life plan and I must determine just how much effort to give at a task. It seemed to me that this way of thinking required a belief in something other than myself.

"I'm not in this alone am I?"

"It is my belief that none of us are. Everything that happens to you, seemingly good or bad, happens for a reason. The reason always has a beneficial component to it if we stop to see it." Jack replied.

I realized that I needed to pay attention to my life purpose; why I lived. It was not my job to try to figure it out; it was my job to carry it out. Goals, on the other hand, were how I lived. I needed to set them and do all I could to accomplish them. It might not happen that I would accomplish all of my stated goals, but if I did not then I should look to see if they conflicted with my life purpose. If they did, I needed to realign these goals. If, on the other hand, I did not reach goals that were in sync with my life purpose, I should look at my effort. Perhaps I needed to reapply myself and attempt the goal again or move on to something else.

The Lessons from Jack

Feeling the need to organize my notes, I began to write down the things I'd learned from Jack. The simple truths of how to succeed seemed to flow from my pen. After a few minutes I'd distilled the hours of conversation into 15 lessons.

1. *Never prejudge a person.* A box has twelve sides, not four, and people are far more complex than they seem. My sitting next to Jack had been a turning point in my life and to think I wanted to change my seat selection! For the rest of my life I would do my best to become interested in the people around me instead of trying to make them interested in me. Jack made me see the difference when the focus is on others and not on me.

2. *With attainment comes responsibility.* If we strive for a successful life we must be prepared for the responsibility of that success. To do less would cheapen the attainment. Less meaningful accomplishments require little responsibility. As your accomplishments broaden so should your desire to seek to become someone worthy of the position.

3. *Are you in prison or free?* Freedom is attained when we are in control of our attitude and are living a purposeful life. We are in prison if our environment controls our attitude. We must learn to take control of what we think, say and write. If we do less we are working against our life purpose.

4. *One must continually separate the important from the unimportant, thinking about and acting on the important while letting the unimportant go.* Do not wait for a crisis to occur before you realize who and what is really important to you. I'd spent most of my life not knowing the difference. I would be a better competitor, spouse, father and friend because of this principle.

5. *It is unimportant what happens to you in life. What is important is what you do about what happens to you.* I had these turned around big time. I would focus more on my response to the results of events and not so much on my success or failure in attempting the event. Sometimes not winning is superior to winning in the long run. I would take all outcomes as positive.

6. *The conscious mind can only think of one thing at a time.* Control your thoughts and you control your attitude and your actions. You have to think about being unhappy to be unhappy. I vowed to focus my conscious thoughts on what I wanted to happen in my life and not worry so much about what I feared might happen.

7. *Everything we experience in life acts as preparation for the future.* My silver medal experience prompted me to begin to search out the secrets of mental control under pressure. That search would result in my developing a system for mental control that would allow me to attain the highest titles my sport could award.

8. ***Your environment is not reality. Your perception of your environment is reality.*** Compared to Jack's imprisonment, my life had been pleasant and without serious challenge. Jack had an environment that was negative and yet he had a positive attitude. I had an environment that was mostly positive and yet I had a negative attitude. In the future, I would choose to perceive my environment as happy and positive and that would alter both my mood and my performance.

9. ***Focus only on the solution to the problem and not on the problem itself.*** Thinking about problems enhances the tension and leads to a depressed attitude. Solutions empower our thinking and energize us.

10. ***Every time you vividly picture doing something you create a preset in your self-image that improves the chances that you will act that way in the future.*** The thousands of imagined perfect golf shots empowered Jack to play almost perfect golf upon his return.

11. ***No matter how bad our environment seems, others have endured more and complained less.*** We should follow their example. I promised myself that I would remember how easy I had it.

12. ***We will not continue to think about a goal if there are not open doors waiting for us to go through that make the goal attainable.*** The gold medal called to me daily. I would not let it go. I would make the next

Olympic team and the gold medal would be mine.

13. ***My job is not to try to direct life's events as much as it is to manage the quality of my own participation in the events.*** I could see the difference between my life purpose that was being controlled by an all-powerful creator and my life goals that were up to me to accomplish.

14. ***Attainment is the best way to measure success not just accomplishment alone.*** In the future, I would evaluate my efforts both in terms of what I had accomplished and in whom I had become.

15. ***God endows us with weapons to fight through adversity.*** I might never know the adversity that Jack and his fellow POWs had faced but I knew that because of them I could see the evidence of God working in man. More than anything else, Jack had taken away my self-pity and replaced it with resolve and confidence.

As I picked my head up from my notes Jack just smiled at me. He reminded me of the way my father would look at me when I'd done something well. I'd gotten the message and Jack knew it. In a few minutes the plane touched down in Cairo and my time with him came to an end.

The United States team would win the Military World Championships that year with Jack Sands as our team captain. I won the individual event aiding my team in setting world records. At the awards ceremony all of our teammates, laden with medals around our necks, had nothing but praise for our experience in Cairo. But for me, this had been much more than a competition. It had been a turning point. I couldn't help but notice that everyone on our team had a medal around his neck but Jack. They don't give medals to team captains. On impulse, I removed one of my medals from around my neck and handed it to Jack.

"You deserve this." I said. "Please accept it. It would mean a lot to me if you did."

"It would be my honor and I will treasure it," Jack said.

Thirty Years Later

Thirty years have passed since the flight to Cairo. I lost track of Jack until just recently. My life has been influenced by the lessons of the box in countless ways.

For two years after I met Jack, I would search for the secrets of mental control under pressure. I interviewed countless Olympic Gold Medalists to determine what they were doing about their mental game. What they told me was truly amazing. I upgraded to it and began to dominate my sport. Jack was right about my being able to return to the marksmanship unit. Although I was told by my assignments officer at the Department of the Army that I could not return to the unit for a full tour of duty it did not preclude my applying for brief periods just prior to the World and Olympic Tryouts. I would become World Champion several times and win my Olympic Gold Medal in the years to follow.

I began an International Shooting School after the Olympic win and over the next decade trained several Olympic and World champions. I coached in two Olympics. I started Mental Management® Systems, a mental-performance-enhancement company, and trained athletes from more than 20 countries, including the Olympic teams of Australia, Korea, Japan, Mexico, Canada, India, the Republic of China and the USA.

For a two-year period, while still in the Army, I was unable to go to a shooting range to train. I remembered how Jack imprinted his golf game in the solitude of the box. We had a bedroom in our home that we were not using. I set up my rifle in this room. At night after my family had retired to bed I would enter this room and practice for several hours. Sometimes, just as Jack had experienced in the box, I would turn out the lights and in total darkness I imagined I was competing and winning.

In a special way, I was in my box. I imprinted thousands of tens and won countless competitions in that room. I controlled my attitude just as Jack had taught me many years before. I knew that my competition would not be training in this special way. It compensated for my not being able to actually shoot. As I look back on it now, I'm convinced that it gave me a huge advantage. I saw only tens. If I'd been actually shooting some of the shots might not have been tens and I would have imprinted them.

Soon after my "box experience," I separated from the army and qualified for the World Championships in Seoul Korea. Many of the shooters were surprised to see me there. One asked me if I thought I had a chance to win the world championship given that I'd not won any of the preliminary competitions. I told him that my chances were excellent because I'd won thousands of preliminaries. I'd won them in my box. I would win the World Championship that year by one of the highest margins in history.

Over the years I've told Jack's story thousands of times. I've done seminars all over the world on my system of mental control called mental management and Jack's principles are an inspiration to this program. Recently, while at the National Championships in rifle shooting, I told Jack's Freedom Flight story to a group of young shooters and coaches. At the break, a coach told me that he not only knew Jack, but he'd just talked to him on his cell phone. Jack had retired from the Navy and was working at the United States Naval Academy in public relations. The coach asked me if I'd like to talk to Jack. I jumped at the chance and in a few minutes I had Jack Sands on the other end of the line.

"Sir." I said, even though both of us were civilians. "Do you remember me?"

"Of course. I've watched your career with great interest. Congratulations on your titles. I understand that your sons are also champion shooters," Jack said.

"Yes, that's right. In fact, Troy has just won the Nationals again. I've thought about you many times over the years and the impact that you've had on my life."

"The fact that you acted on the principles resulted in the impact, not me. You were ready to learn and the plan supplied the teacher. It always works like that you know," Jack replied.

"Yes, I know. But I just wanted to thank you again for your story and the actions you took on my behalf. It is so powerful. Have you ever written a book or created a course based on your experiences?" I asked.

There was a pause in the phone. Then Jack said, "That's not my job." Then another pause. "It's yours."

Looking back on my life I'm convinced that things happen for a reason. Sometimes life hands us adversity to teach us valuable lessons to be used in the future. Sometimes we are fortunate to learn from the adversity of others. Jack will never forget his freedom flight but I

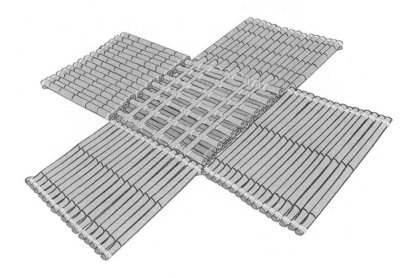

am just as certain that I will not forget mine. It was my Freedom Flight on that trip to Cairo. I was set free. Free from focusing on the unimportant at the expense of the important. Free from prejudging others. Free to allow the important things about my life to guide my attitude and let go of the unimportant. Free to focus on solutions and not on the problems. Free to trust in God, that He is there for me and that I am never alone. Jack helped me to understand that I had been in prison without knowing it; the prison of living life without a purpose. He helped me to see that once I found my life purpose that the walls of my box would come down. Every time I see an airplane, a wristwatch or a box I'm reminded of Jack and I rejoice that I am no longer in prison. I'm free!

About Freedom Flight

Freedom Flight – The Origins of Mental Power is inspired by true events. All of the references to Lanny Bassham are accurate as presented. Jack Sands is based on three extraordinary men; Major William L. Bassham USA (Lanny's Father), LTC Bill Pullum USA (Coach of USAMU International Rifle Section), CPT Jack Fellowes USN (the POW team captain of the US Shooting Team that competed in Cairo in 1974) and the experiences of other POWs. The conversations are a dramatization and certain liberties were taken for effect but the principles and influences are those of real people as they affected the attainment of the events of the story.

WITH WINNING IN MIND

(200 page 3rd. Edition)

The book that started it all, great for anyone interested in having a consistent mental performance under pressure. The book introduces Mental Management and is packed with techniques for competitors. Learn how performance is a function of three mental processes, how to control the mind under pressure and how to train for competition. Unlock the secrets of Olympic Champions. **$16.95**

WITH WINNING IN MIND

(AUDIO CD - includes 2 audio CDs)

With Winning In Mind is great for anyone interested in having a consistent mental performance under pressure. The book introduces Mental Management and is packed with techniques for competitors. Learn how performance is a function of three mental processes, how to control the mind under pressure and how to train for competition. Unlock the secrets of Olympic Champions. Includes bonus CD with over 50 minutes of added material. **$35**

http://www.mentalmanagement.com

Lanny Bassham, founder of Mental Mangement Systems, is the driving force behind the creation of the mental strategies presented in the seminars and products offered by the company.

Lanny not only developed the Mental Management System but also used it personally to win 35 medals in international rifle competition for the USA including 22 world individual and team titles, setting 4 world records and winning the coveted Olympic Gold Medal in Montreal in 1976. This ranks him third in medal count for the USA among all shooters. Lanny is a member of the USA Shooting Hall of Fame. He lives in Flower Mound, Texas.

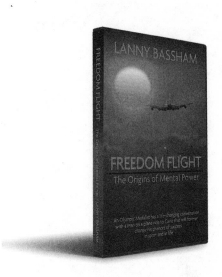

Order Freedom Flight
in hardcover or in audio CD from
Mental Management Systems
1-800-879-5079
www.mentalmanagement.com